Jeff Abell
Oct 2012

composition in retrospect

D1547327

JOHN CAGE

composition in retrospect

1993 EXACT CHANGE CAMBRIDGE

©1982, 1983, 1993 John Cage

This edition ©1993 Exact Change
Published by arrangement with the author

All Rights Reserved
ISBN 978-1-878972-11-1

Cover illustration by John Cage

Exact Change books are edited by Damon Krukowski
and designed by Naomi Yang

Exact Change
5 Brewster Street
Cambridge, MA 02138
www.exactchange.com

Distributed by D.A.P. / Distributed Art Publishers
155 Sixth Avenue, 2nd floor, New York, NY 10013
www.artbook.com

Printed on acid-free, responsibly harvested
(FSC certified) and/or recycled paper

publisher's note

Composition in Retrospect was started in 1981 and completed in 1988. In 1983 the first portion of it was included in John Cage's book *X*, and his original introduction to it is reprinted here. The expanded text appeared in a different form as part of the source material for the Norton Lectures delivered at Harvard in 1988–1989, printed in 1990 under the title *I-VI*. In early 1992 Exact Change asked John Cage if he would like to collect any of his recent writings for a new book; he replied yes, he would like to print an integral edition of *Composition in Retrospect* in its original mesostic form. At first he said he was going to add to it further, but in July he wrote and said that he would not continue the piece after all, that he had just read it to an audience in Europe and "it seems to carry me to where I am at present." He asked that it be accompanied by *Themes and Variations*, a piece written in 1980 and first published in 1982. One of his works on paper was selected to illustrate the cover.

In August 1992 John Cage died at the age of seventy-nine. Exact Change has made every effort to present this work as he had requested. It is published with the gracious cooperation of Merce Cunningham and Laura Kuhn.

For those unfamiliar with John Cage's writings, the following explanation of the mesostic form is taken from his introduction to the Norton Lectures: "Like acrostics, mesostics are written in the conventional way horizontally, but at the same time they follow a vertical rule, down the middle not down the edge as in an acrostic, a string which spells a word or name, not necessarily connected with what is being written, though it may be. This vertical rule is lettristic and in my practice the letters are capitalized. Between two capitals in a perfect or 100% mesostic neither letter may appear in lower case. In an imperfect or 50% mesostic the first letter may reappear but the second one is not permitted until its appearance on the second line as a capital in the string. . . . In the writing of the wing words, the horizontal text, the letters of the vertical string help me out of sentimentality. I have something to do, a puzzle to solve. This way of responding makes me feel in this respect one with the Japanese people, who formerly, I once learned, turned their letter writing into the writing of poems."

The explanation continues with a statement that applies to the composition of *Themes and Variations* and to the chance-determined stanzas of *Composition in Retrospect:* "In taking the next step in my work, the exploration of non-intention, I don't solve the puzzle that the mesostic string presents. Instead I write or find a source text which is then used as an oracle. I ask it what word shall I use for this letter and what one for the next, etc. This frees me from memory, taste, likes and dislikes. . . . With respect to the source material, I am in a global situation. Words come first from here and then from there. The situation is not linear. It is as though I am in a forest hunting for ideas."

composition in retrospect

introduction

This text has twelve short parts,* each made up of seven mesostics, the first six of which make sense. The last does not do so conventionally: it is a chance-determined mix of the preceding six. *Composition in Retrospect* was written as part of an intensive international workshop for professional choreographers and composers conducted in August 1981 by Merce Cunningham and myself at the University of Surrey in Guildford, England. What happened was that from nine to ten-thirty in the morning I spoke in an informal way on an aspect of my composition; from ten-thirty to eleven there was a tea and coffee break during which the composers received specific assignments for that evening's performance of music and dance; from eleven to twelve-thirty I composed that part of the following text that was related to my earlier talk in the presence of those members of the workshop who chose to be with me. This continued for two weeks, six days a week. On the first day I found I could not write more than six mesostics. I then took six as the number that had to be written each of the following days.

*This introduction was written in 1983; in 1988 *Composition in Retrospect* was expanded from twelve to seventeen parts. (Publisher's note)

composition in retrospect

My
mEmory
of whaT
Happened
is nOt
what happeneD

i aM struck
by thE
facT
tHat what happened
is mOre conventional
than what i remembereD

iMitations
invErsions
reTrograde forms
motives tHat are varied
Or
not varieD

once Music
bEgins
iT remains
He said the same
even variatiOn is repetition
some things changeD others not (schoenberg)

what i aM
rEmembering
incorrecTly to be sure
is wHatever
deviated frOm
orDinary practice

not a scale or row but a gaMut
to Each
elemenT
of wHich
equal hOnor
coulD be given

iMitations
invErsions
iT remains
motives tHat are varied
deviated frOm
than what i remembereD

the diviSion of a whole
inTo
paRts
dUration
not frequenCy
Taken
as the aspect of soUnd
bRinging about
a distinction bEtween

both phraSes
and large secTions
many diffeRent distinctions
coUld be thought of
some for instanCe
concerning symmeTry horizontal or vertical
bUt what i thought of
was a Rhythmic
structurE

in which the Small
parTs
had the same pRoportion to each other
that the groUps of units the large parts had to the whole
for instanCe
64 since iT
eqUals eight eights
peRmits
division of both sixty-four and Each eight into three two and three

        in *Songe d'une*
         nuiT d'été
  satie divided fouR
            foUrs into one two and one (four eight and four)
    and in other pieCes
he worked symmeTrically
        coUnting
      the numbeR
        bEtween

         Succeeding numbers
    following addiTion six plus two
      with subtRaction
      six minUs two
    and/or reaChing
         a cenTer of a series of phrases
        continUing
  by going backwaRds
        six Eight

        four Seven five
    seven four eighT six six being
        the centeR horizontally five vertically
        thUs
        a Canvas
         of Time is provided hospitable to both noise
      and mUsical tones upon which
  music may be dRawn
      spacE

                in which the Small
                      inTo
            the centeR horizontally five vertically
                    foUrs into one two and one (four eight and four)
            and/or reaChing
                      of Time is provided hospitable to both noise
as the aspect of soUnd
                    peRmits
        a distinction bEtween

                    musIc
                for the daNce
                        To go with it
                    to Express
                the daNce in sound
                    noT
                    beIng able
                    tO do
            the same thiNg

                        gIves the possibility
                of doiNg
                someThing
            that diffErs
                    liviNg
                in The same town
                    fInding life
                by nOt
                    liviNg the same way

9

the dancers from malaysIa
a theatrical crossiNg
from lefT to right
so slowly as to sEem to be
moviNg
noT at all
the musIc meanwhile
as fast as pOssible
togetherNess

of opposItes
purposeful purposelessNess
noT
to accEpt it
uNless i could remain
aT
the same tIme
a member Of society
able to fulfill a commissioN

to satIsfy
a particular Need
Though having no control
ovEr
what happeNs
accepTance
sometImes
written Out
determiNate

sometImes
just a suggestioN
i found iT
workEd
therefore i Nap
pounding The
rIce
withOut
liftiNg my hand

gIves the possibility
a theatrical crossiNg
Though having no control
that diffErs
uNless i could remain
in The same town
the same tIme
as fast as pOssible
togetherNess

to sober and quiet the minD
so that It
iS
in aCcord
wIth
what haPpens
the worLd
around It
opeN
rathEr than

closeD
goIng in
by Sitting
Crosslegged
returnIng
to daily exPerience
with a smiLe
gIft
giviNg no why
aftEr emptiness

he saiD
It
iS
Complete
goes full cIrcle the structure of the mind
Passes
from the absoLute
to the world of relatIvity
perceptioNs
during thE

Day and dreams
at nIght
Suzuki
the magiC square
and then chance operatIons
going out through sense Perceptions
to foLlow a metal ball
away from lIkes
aNd
dislikEs

throw it on the roaD
                fInd it in my ear
         the Shaggy nag
     now after suCcess
take your sword and slIt my throat
           the Prince hesitates
      but not for Long
lo and behold the nag Immediately
     becomes agaiN
     the princE

      he haD
          orIginally been and would never have again become
had the other refuSed to kill him
       silenCe
       sweepIng fallen leaves
       sweePing up
         Leaves three years later
suddenly understood saId
       thaNk you
     again no rEply

to sober and quiet the minD
         goIng in
       iS
     in aCcord
   returnIng
going out through sense Perceptions
    with a smiLe
lo and behold the nag Immediately
    becomes agaiN
       aftEr emptiness

he sent us to the blackboarD
and asked us to solve a problem In counterpoint
even though it waS
a Class
In harmony
to make as many counterPoints
as we couLd
after each to let hIm see it
that's correct Now
anothEr

after eight or nine solutions i saiD
not quIte
Sure of myself there aren't any more
that's Correct
now I want you
to Put in words
the principLe
that underlIes
all of the solutioNs
hE

haD always seemed to me
superIor
to other human beingS
but then my worship of him inCreased even more
I couldn't do what he asked
Perhaps now
thirty years Later
I
caN
i think hE

woulD agree
the prInciple
underlying all of the Solutions
aCts
In the question that is asked
as a comPoser
i shouLd
gIve up
makiNg
choicEs

Devote myself
to askIng
queStions
Chance
determIned
answers'll oPen
my mind to worLd around
at the same tIme
chaNging my music
sElf-alteration not self-expression

thoreau saiD the same
thIng
over a hundred yearS ago
i want my writing to be as Clear
as water I can see through
so that what i exPerienced
is toLd
wIthout
my beiNg in any way
in thE way

Devote myself
(superIor)
to other human beingS
a Class
now I want you
so that what i exPerienced
is toLd
I
my beiNg in any way
choicEs

he maDe
an arrangement of objects In front of them
and aSked the students
to Concentrate
attentIon on it
until it was Part
and parceL
of hIs or her thoughts
theN
to go to thE wall

which he haD covered
wIth paper
to place both noSe and toes
in Contact
wIth it
keePing that contact
and using charcoaL
to draw the Image
which each had iN mind
all thE

stuDents
were In
poSitions
that disConnected
mInd and hand
the drawings were suddenly contemPorary
no Longer
fIxed
iN
tastE

anD
preconceptIon
the collaboration with oneSelf
that eaCh person
conventIonally
Permits
had been made impossibLe
by a physIcal
positioN
anothEr

crossleggeDness
the result of whIch
iS rapid transportation
eaCh student
had wanted to become a modern artIst
Put out of touch
with himseLf
dIscovery
suddeN
opEning

                    of Doors
                      It
                    waS
                      a Class
                      gIven by mark tobey
        in the same Part
        of the worLd
                      I walked with him from school
              to chiNatown
                      hE was always stopping pointing out things to see

        which he haD covered
                  was In
    and place both noSe and toes
                    to Concentrate
                    mInd and hand
          in the same Part
          with himseLf
                      I walked with him from school
              suddeN
              anothEr

                  turNing the paper
                    intO
              a space of Time
    imperfections in the pAper upon which
                    The
                      musIc is written
      the music is there befOre
                    it is writteN

compositioN
is Only making
iT
cleAr
That that
Is the case
finding Out
a simple relatioN

betweeN paper and music
hOw
To
reAd
iT
Independently
Of
oNe's thoughts

what iNstrument
Or
insTruments
stAff
or sTaves
the possIbility
Of
a microtoNal music

more space betweeN staff lines representing
majOr
Thirds
thAn minor
so That
If
a nOte
has No

                accideNtal
it is between well-knOwn
                poinTs in the field of frequency
        or just A drawing in space
                piTch
            vertIcally
    time reading frOm left to right
                abseNce of theory

                accideNtal
            majOr
                To
            stAff
                The
            vertIcally
        finding Out
                oNe's thoughts

    you can't be serIous she said
        we were driNking
            a recorD
            was bEing played
                noT
            in thE place
            wheRe we were
but in another rooM
                I had
            fouNd it interesting
                And had asked
        what musiC it was
        not to supplY

a partIcular photograph
but to thiNk
of materials that woulD
makE
iT
possiblE
foR
soMeone else
to make hIs
owN
A
Camera
it was necessarY

for davId tudor
somethiNg
a puzzle that he woulD
solvE
Taking
as a bEginning
what was impossible to measuRe
and then returning what he could to Mystery
It was
while teachiNg
A
Class
at wesleYan

that I thought
of Number II
i haD
bEen explaining
variaTions
onE
suddenly Realized
that two notations on the saMe
pIece of paper
automatically briNg
About relationship
my Composing
is actuallY unnecessary

musIc
Never stops it is we who turn away
again the worlD around
silEnce
sounds are only bubbles on iTs
surfacE
they buRst to disappear (thoreau)
when we Make
musIc
we merely make somethiNg
thAt
Can
more naturallY be heard than seen or touched

that makes It possible
to pay atteNtion
to Daily work or play
as bEing
noT
what wE think it is
but ouR goal
all that's needed is a fraMe
a change of mental attItude
amplificatioN
wAiting for a bus
we're present at a Concert
suddenlY we stand on a work of art the pavement

musIc
Never stops it is we who turn away
i haD
as bEing
noT
surfacE
foR
all that's needed is a fraMe
It was
amplificatioN
wAiting for a bus
my Composing
not to supplY

musIcircus
maNy
Things going on
at thE same time
a theatRe of differences together
not a single Plan
just a spacE of time
aNd
as many pEople as are willing
performing in The same place
a laRge
plAce a gymnasium
an archiTecture
that Isn't
invOlved
with makiNg the stage

dIrectly opposite
the audieNce and higher
Thus
morE
impoRtant than where they're sitting
the resPonsibility
of Each
persoN *is*
marcEl duchamp said
To complete
the woRk himself
to heAr
To see
orIginally
we need tO
chaNge

not only archItecture

but the relatioN

of arT

to monEy

theRe will be too many musicians

to Pay

thE

eveNt

must bE free

To the public

heRe

As elsewhere

we find That

socIety needs

tO be

chaNged

I

thiNk

That

many of our problEms will be solved

if we take advantage of buckminsteR fuller's

Plans

for thE

improvemeNt

of the circumstancEs of our lives

an equaTion

between woRld resources

And human needs

so That

It

wOrks

for everyoNe

not just the rIch
No
naTions
to bEgin with
and no goveRnment at all (thoreau also said this)
an intelligent Plan
that will hEal
the preseNt
schizophrEnia
The use
of eneRgy sources
Above
earTh
not fossIl fuels
quickly air will imprOve
aNd water too

not the promIse
of giviNg us
arTificial
Employment
but to use ouR technology
Producing
a sociEty
based on unemploymeNt
thE purpose
of invenTion
has always been to diminish woRk
we now hAve
The
possIbility
tO become a society
at oNe with itself

not just the rIch
of giviNg us
That
at thE same time
theRe will be too many musicians
to Plan
a sociEty
the eveNt
thE purpose
To the public
has always been to diminish woRk
Above
The
not fossIl fuels
we need tO
chaNge

the past must be Invented
the future Must be
revIsed
doing boTh
mAkes
whaT
the present Is
discOvery
Never stops

what questIons
will Make the past
alIve
in anoTher
wAy
in The case
of satIe's
sOcrate
seeiNg

It
as polyModal
(modal chromatIcally)
allowed me To
Ask
of all The modes
whIch?
Of
the twelve toNes

whIch?
renovation of Melody
In
The
cAse
of eighTeenth-century hymns
knowIng the number
Of
toNes

In each voice
to ask which of the nuMbers
are passIve
which acTive
these Are
firsT tone
then sIlence
this brings abOut
a harmoNy

a tonalIty
freed froM theory
In *chorals*
of saTie
to chAnge
The staff so there's equal space for each half tone
then rubbIng the twelve
intO
the microtoNal (japan calcutta etcetera)

whIch?
as polyModal
revIsed
allowed me To
these Are
firsT tone
of satIe's
Of
the microtoNal (japan calcutta etcetera)

a month spent failing to finD
a nEw music for piano
haVing characteristics
that wOuld
inTerest grete sultan
fInally left my desk
went tO visit her
she is Not as i am

just concerneD
                    with nEw music
                    she loVes the past
                    the rOom she lives works and
                    Teaches
                    In
               has twO
               piaNos

          she surrounDs
               hErself
with mozart beethoVen bach
               all Of
                    The best of the past
               but lIke buhlig
               whO first played
               schoeNberg's opus eleven

     and also arrangeD
                         thE art of the fugue for two pianos
               she loVes new music
          seeing nO real difference
               beTween
          some of It
and the classics she's sO devoted to
               theN

          i noticeD
               hEr hands
          conceiVed a duet
               fOr
                    Two hands each alone
          then catalogued all of the Intervals triads and aggregates
a single hand can play unassisted by the Other
               sooN

30

finisheD
thE first of thirty-two études
each haVing
twO pages
showed iT to grete
she was delIghted
that was eight years agO
the first performaNce of all thirty-two will be given next year

she surrounDs
thE art of the fugue for two pianos
each haVing
that wOuld
showed iT to grete
she was delIghted
whO first played
sooN

aCt
In
accoRd
with obstaCles
Using
theM
to find or define the proceSs
you're abouT to be involved in
the questions you'll Ask
if you doN't have enough time
to aCcomplish
what you havE in mind
conSider the work finished

onCe
It is begun
it then Resembles the venus de milo
whiCh manages so well
withoUt
an arM
divide the work to be done into partS
and the Time
Available
iNto an equal number
then you Can
procEed giving equal attention
to each of the partS

or you Could say
study beIng
inteRrupted
take telephone Calls
as Unexpected pleasures
free the Mind
from itS desire
To
concentrAte
remaiNing open
to what you Can't
prEdict
"i welcome whatever happenS next"

if you're writing a pieCe for orchestra
and you know what the copyIng costs
                    aRe
                    suCh
                and sUch
            take the aMount of money
you've been promiSed
            and divide iT to determine
        the number of pAges
            of your Next
                        Composition
            this will givE you
            the canvaS

            upon whiCh
you're about to wrIte
            howeveR
                    aCceptance of whatever
                    mUst
                be coMplemented
        by the refuSal
            of everyThing
                thAt's
                    iNtolerable
        revolution Can
                nEver
                Stop

even though eaCh
mornIng
we awake with eneRgy
(niChi nichi kore ko nichi)
and as individUals
can solve any probleM
that confrontS us
we musT do the impossible
rid the world of nAtions
briNging
the play of intelligent anarChy
into a world Environment
that workS so well everyone lives as he needs

upon whiCh
It is begun
howeveR
aCceptance of whatever
mUst
can solve any probleM
to find or define the proceSs
of everyThing
Available
iNtolerable
Composition
procEed giving equal attention
"i welcome whatever happenS next"

for some time now i haVe been using
time-brAckets
sometimes they aRe
fIxed
And sometimes not
By fixed
i mean they begin and end at particuLar
points in timE

when there are not pointS
                    Time
                        foR both beginnings and endings is in space
                the sitUation
            is muCh more flexible
                    These time-brackets
                are Used
            in paRts
        parts for which thEre is no score no fixed relationship

it was part i thought of a moVement in composition
                    Away
                fRom structure
                Into process
                Away
            from an oBject having parts
        into what you might caLl
                wEather

                    now i See
                    That
            the time bRackets
                took Us
                    baCk from
                        weaTher which had been reached to object
        they made an earthqUake
                    pRoof music
                so to spEak

music the parts of which can moVe with respect to
eAch
otheR
It is not entirely
structurAl
But it is at the same time not
entireLy
frEe

of partS
differenT composing means
aRe
Used
a b and C
a is a non repeTitive passage within a given range
b is nothing bUt a single tone
silence aRound it
rEpeated any number of times

c is the prescribed use of fiVe tones
A gamut
which eitheR
remaIns is immobile
or is mobile chAnges music for
if instead of a B and c
there's onLy a
wEather

                    iS
              whaT happens
                 pRocess
                    Undivided happens
                    Changing
              in iTs way
              withoUt
              cleaRly
                    sEparated parts

          what do you haVe
                 to sAy
              about Rhythm
          let us agree It is no longer
                    A question of patterns
                    But patterns
              couLd
              arisE

              and diSappear
     no need for such agreemenT
                    Rhythm is
          coexistence of dUrations of any length
              durations in suCcession
          and synchroniciTy
                    sUccession is liveliest when
          as in feldman's woRk
              it is not fixEd

                    37

but within a giVen period of time
in situAtion
foRm
It is presented
entrAnces
Being
at any point in time at aLl
this is this momEnt quoted

from Silence
synchroniciTy is liveliest
most unpRedictably changing
when the parts are Unfixed
by a sCore
no Two performances
yielding the same resUltant
duRations
that was thirty-thrEe years ago

music the parts of which can moVe with respect to
time-brAckets
foRm
It is presented
Away
But it is at the same time not
entireLy
wEather

and diSappear
buT spaces of time
most unpRedictably changing
coexistence of dUrations of any length
by a sCore
no Two performances
b is nothing bUt a single tone
in paRts
it is not fixEd

people ofteN ask what music
i prefer tO hear
i eNjoy
the absence of mUsic
more thaN any other
or you coulD say
silEnce
i enjoy whateveR
ambient Sounds
There
Are to hear what i like
is that they areN't saying anything
they just Do what
It is they are
i listeN
no matter in what else i happen to be enGaged

experieNce
nOt
kNowing what will happen next
i am of coUrse
a percussioN composer
what i wanteD to do was to find a way
not to know what thE beat was even though
what i'd wRite
would be meaSured
make The
meAsure
loNg twelve to fifteen beats
only five of which were to be hearD
slow the tempo down to sIxty
you caN't in metrical terms ryoanji
understand what you're hearinG

aNy
mOre
thaN
yoU
caN when you
listen to ambient sounD
traffic for instancE
i decided to go fuRthur
in thiS
direcTion etc 2/4 orchs
keeping 5 icti i doubled the number of beAts per measure (27 - 36)
at the same time reduciNg the tempi to
such slow speeDs that they became
chronometrIc
somethiNg
for which you couldn't have a feelinG except through the ear

we are iN
the wOrld of duchamp
souNds lasting leaving from
different points in space mUsical sculpture
collectioN of rocks
when will the sounD
changE
there is no way eveR to know
Surrounded
by mysTery
reAlity
what is clear'N'concise
joyce saiD
can't deal wIth reality
we are iN the dark
we are losinG

our miNds getting mind
it is as thOugh
souNds
occUr
of their owN
accorD
wE
aRe no longer
Supervising
To
whAt
leNgths
Do
I go
there is No
stoppinG

or goiNg
        O
    mooN
why are yoU so willow tree?
        maNy
        sounDs?
        wE
    can neveR know
        if So
            The end
            A book
        of iNstructions
    what to Do
        to take It apart
                aNd put it back up
                áGain nohopera

            aNy
        it is as thOugh
            thaN
        no mUsic
    more thaN any other
    what i wanteD to do was to find a way
traffic for instancE
        what i'd wRite
            ambient Sounds
            made The
            whAt
                loNg twelve to fifteen beats
        joyce saiD
    chronometrIc
                aNd put it back up
    we are losinG

musiC resulting
frOm
a separatioN
of cause and effecT
a conch shell partIally filled with water
time speNt
tippinG it
first onE way
aNd then another
you may notiCe
shells are verY temperamental

mostly no sounds take plaCe silence
sOmetimes
oN
The other hand
It's easy
the shell speaks coNtinuously
a Gurgling
voicE
amplificatioN's required
for it to be heard by an audienCe
at anY

distanCe
shells Of
differiNg sizes
Three players
an Improvised music
over which No one has control
thouGh
Each
musiciaN's
aCtion
is necessarY

an old flimsy musiC stand
made Of metal
driveN upside down
across The floor
ears are tourIsts
oNce
aGain
thE
musiciaN
has no Control
no waY to know what sound he'll make and when

musiC written
fOr
percussioN
buT
wIthout
Names for instruments
just numberinG
thEm
this briNgs
about a musiC
not in anY way

antiCipated
by the cOmposer
though without his writiNg
iT
It
wouldN't happen
not lookinG for
othEr breaks
betweeN
Cause and effect
just remaining readY

musiC written
sOmetimes
though without his writiNg
Three players
wIthout
Names for instruments
thouGh
othEr breaks
this briNgs
aCtion
shells are verY temperamental

to avoId
the paralyziNg
effeCts
Of
experieNce
to uSe
the mInd
in four different wayS
arTha
thE world
of success aNd failure
the Concern
alwaYs not to

fall
but to wiN not to die but to live
kama to aCt
in terms Of
pleasure and paiN
giving pleaSure
not paIn
Sex
and arT
thE beautiful
is oNly
what Clicks for
You

keep a clIcker
iN
your poCket wittgenstein
just in case yOu
eNcounter
uglineSs that needs
transformatIon
uglineSs
That
aftEr
oNe
Click
You accept

as beautIful
                    traNsformation
          sudden Change
                    Of
                    miNd
the third india iS dharma
          good'n'evIl
          true'n'falSe
                    righT'n'wrong
          in thE
          moral seNse
                    disCrimination
following in a general waY

          the buddhIst
          the christiaN
          the islamiC
                    Or
          the aNy other
          outlineS
                    of lIfe'n'action
finally mokSha
          liberaTion
                    thE flower the smile
          the returN bearing gifts to the village
freedom from Concern
concerns that return before You can say you're free

these varIous ways
of usiNg
one's faCulties
cOexist
iNterpenetrate
producing i am not Sure
I am
Surprised
how can you say That you just said this
whEther
determiNate or indeterminate
Conducted or not
purposeless purpose waY the way

these varIous ways
iN
the islamiC
in terms Of
miNd
the third india iS dharma
of lIfe'n'action
uglineSs
liberaTion
aftEr
moral seNse
Conducted or not
You

Practicality action is action
thE metal ones
won't buRn
wooden statues oF the buddha winter fire
quick O quick
a woRd of truth
one arM
holding the cAt
the other the kNife
quiCk
or i slit thE cat's throat

what you have doesn't helP
lEss
is moRe
Feathers
pulled Out
gRadual
iMprovement
it needs A
loNg time
but like thunderClap
its own timE no time at all

Punctuation
its rEmoval
the Removal
oF the curtain
cOnstant
theatRe
poetry contest life is a Mirror it collects dust
problem is removAl of the dust
that is Not a good poem
what would you write i Can't
writE

                        sixth Patriarch
                  so tEll us what you would say
              what miRror what dust
          in the middle oF the night
        the fifth take this rObe this bowl
                        oR whatever these are
                        My
                  insigniA they are yours
              escape this Night
          as fast as you Can
                        thEy'll come after you

        they did they caught uP with him
                        dEmanded
                  the Robe the bowl
                  he oFfered them
                  withOut hesitation
          placing them on the Rock
              between theM
          but they were unAble
                  eveN
                  to touCh
                        thE robe the bowl

                  let alone Pick
                  thEm up
                  theRe is no dust
                        iF there isn't any dust
              why are yOu always taking baths
              centuRies later no reason
                        My dips're dips
                  just A dip
                  No why
                  no Causing
                  of Effects what effects are these

                              50

they did they caught uP with him
                    lEss
               the Removal
               he oFfered them
     the fifth take this rObe this bowl
                    centuRies later no reason
               one arM
               insigniA they are yours
                    loNg time
what would you write i Can't
                    thE robe the bowl

themes & variations

introduction

The following text was written to be spoken outloud. It consists of five sections, each to take twelve minutes. The fourth is the fastest and the last one is the slowest.

There are fifteen themes. They are mesostics on the names of fifteen men who have been important to me in my life and work: Norman O. Brown, Marshall McLuhan, Erik Satie, Robert Rauschenberg, Buckminster Fuller, Marcel Duchamp, Jasper Johns, Henry David Thoreau, James Joyce, Merce Cunningham, David Tudor, Morris Graves, Mark Tobey, Arnold Schoenberg, Suzuki Daisetz. Many more could be added to this list. But to make a twelve minute talk I needed no more than fifteen and I took those who first came to mind.

Ordinarily when I write mesostics, I write about the person whose name is a row going down the middle of the text, though some are a collection of mesostics "re and not re" that person. The mesostics in this text are exceptionally not about the men named at all, except coincidentally. Instead they are derived from three, four, or five mesostics of equal length written on any of the following one hundred and ten ideas which I listed in the course of a cursory examination of my books (*Virgil Thomson: His Music,* part of a book otherwise written by Kathleen O'Donnell Hoover; *Silence; A Year from Monday; M;* and *Empty Words*).

NONINTENTION (THE ACCEPTANCE OF SILENCE) LEADING TO NATURE; RENUNCIATION OF CONTROL; LET SOUNDS BE SOUNDS.

EACH ACTIVITY IS CENTERED IN ITSELF, I.E., COMPOSITION, PERFORMANCE, AND LISTENING ARE DIFFERENT ACTIVITIES.

(MUSIC IS) INSTANTANEOUS AND UNPREDICTABLE; NOTHING IS ACCOMPLISHED BY WRITING, HEARING, OR PLAYING A PIECE OF MUSIC; OUR EARS ARE NOW IN EXCELLENT CONDITION.

A NEED FOR POETRY.

JOYCE: "COMEDY IS THE GREATEST OF ARTS BECAUSE THE JOY OF COMEDY IS FREEST FROM DESIRE AND LOATHING."

AFFIRMATION OF LIFE.

PURPOSEFUL PURPOSELESSNESS.

ART = IMITATION OF NATURE IN HER MANNER OF OPERATION.

COEXISTENCE OF DISSIMILARS; MULTIPLICITY; PLURALITY OF CENTERS; "SPLIT THE STICK, AND THERE IS JESUS."

ANONYMITY OR SELFLESSNESS OF WORK (I.E., NOT SELF-EXPRESSION).

A WORK SHOULD INCLUDE ITS ENVIRONMENT, IS ALWAYS EXPERIMENTAL (UNKNOWN IN ADVANCE).

FLUENT, PREGNANT, RELATED, OBSCURE (NATURE OF SOUND).

EMPTY MIND.

NO IDEAS OF ORDER.

NO BEGINNING, MIDDLE, OR END (PROCESS, NOT OBJECT).

UNIMPEDEDNESS AND INTERPENETRATION; NO CAUSE AND EFFECT.

INDETERMINACY.

OPPOSITES = PARTS OF ONENESS.

TO THICKEN THE PLOT (RAMAKRISHNA); HIS ANSWER TO THE QUESTION: WHY, IF GOD IS GOOD, IS THERE EVIL IN THE WORLD?

ADVENTURE (NEWNESS) NECESSARY TO CREATIVE ACTION.

IF THE MIND IS DISCIPLINED (BODY TOO), THE HEART TURNS QUICKLY FROM FEAR TOWARDS LOVE (ECKHART).

ANYTHING CAN FOLLOW ANYTHING ELSE (PROVIDING NOTHING IS TAKEN AS THE BASIS).

INFLUENCE DERIVES FROM ONE'S OWN WORK (NOT FROM OUTSIDE IT).

CHANCE OPERATIONS ARE A USEFUL MEANS; MOKSHA.

BEING LED BY A PERSON, NOT A BOOK; ARTHA.

LOVE.

RIGHT AND WRONG.

NON-MEASURED TIME.

PROCESS INSTEAD OF OBJECT.

AMERICA HAS A CLIMATE FOR EXPERIMENTATION.

WORLD IS ONE WORLD.

HISTORY IS THE STORY OF ORIGINAL ACTIONS.

MOVE FROM ZERO.

ALL AUDIBLE PHENOMENA = MATERIAL FOR MUSIC.

IMPOSSIBILITY OF ERRORLESS WORK.

SPRING, SUMMER, FALL, WINTER (CREATION, PRESERVATION, DESTRUCTION, QUIESCENCE).

POSSIBILITY OF HELPING BY DOING NOTHING.

MUSIC IS NOT MUSIC UNTIL IT IS HEARD.

MUSIC AND DANCE TOGETHER (AND THEN OTHER TOGETHERS).

MEN ARE MEN; MOUNTAINS ARE MOUNTAINS BEFORE STUDYING ZEN. WHILE STUDYING ZEN, THINGS BECOME CONFUSED. AFTER STUDYING ZEN, MEN ARE MEN; MOUNTAINS ARE MOUNTAINS. WHAT IS THE DIFFERENCE BETWEEN BEFORE AND AFTER? NO DIFFERENCE. JUST THE FEET ARE A LITTLE OFF THE GROUND (SUZUKI).

IF STRUCTURE, RHYTHMIC STRUCTURE.

BOREDOM PLUS ATTENTION = BECOMING INTERESTED.

PRINCIPLE UNDERLYING ALL OF THE SOLUTIONS = QUESTION WE ASK.

ACTIVITY, NOT COMMUNICATION.

THE NINE PERMANENT EMOTIONS (THE HEROIC, THE MIRTHFUL, THE WONDROUS, THE EROTIC; TRANQUILLITY; SORROW, FEAR, ANGER, THE ODIOUS).

THE PRACTICALITY OF CHANGING SOCIETY DERIVES FROM THE POSSIBILITY OF CHANGING THE MIND.

THE GIVER OF GIFTS (RETURNING TO THE VILLAGE HAVING EXPERIENCED NO-MINDEDNESS).

STUDYING BEING INTERRUPTED.

NOTHING-IN-BETWEEN.

OBJECT IS FACT NOT SYMBOL (NO IDEAS).

POETRY IS HAVING NOTHING TO SAY AND SAYING IT; WE POSSESS NOTHING.

UNCERTAINTY OF FUTURE.

NOISES (UNDERDOG); CHANGING MUSIC AND SOCIETY.

NOT WORKING = KNOWING. WORKING = NOT KNOWING.

DISTRUST OF EFFECTIVENESS OF EDUCATION.

HCE

IT IS, IS CAUSE FOR JOY.

EARTH HAS NO ESCAPE FROM HEAVEN (ECKHART).

Mobility, immobility.

Highest purpose = no purpose. Vision = no vision. (In accord with nature.)

We are the oldest at having our airway of knowing nowness (Gertrude Stein).

Fluency in and out.

No split between spirit and matter.

Importance of being perplexed. Unpredictability.

Not being interrupted by shadows (by environment).

Theatre is closer to life than art or music.

Devotion.

Enlightened = not enlightened. Learning = learning we're not learning.

Breaking rules.

No use for value judgments.

We are all going in different directions.

Importance of no rules.

Going to extremes (Yuji Takahashi).

Absence of boredom.

ANARCHY.

MEANINGLESSNESS AS ULTIMATE MEANING.

MIND CAN CHANGE.

TO DO MORE RATHER THAN LESS.

TO SOBER AND QUIET THE MIND THUS MAKING IT SUSCEPTIBLE TO DIVINE INFLUENCES.

THE MEANS OF THINKING ARE EXTERIOR TO THE MIND.

ART IS CRIMINAL ACTION.

LOVE = LEAVING SPACE AROUND LOVED ONE.

UTILITIES, NOT POLITICS (INTELLIGENCE; PROBLEM SOLVING). ANARCHY IN A PLACE THAT WORKS.

NOT JUST SELF—BUT SOCIAL-REALIZATION.

UNEMPLOYMENT (CF. ARTISTS).

GIVING UP OWNERSHIP, SUBSTITUTING USE.

WHOLE SOCIETY (INCLUDING, E.G., THE MAD: THEY SPEAK THE TRUTH).

RELIGIOUS ATTITUDE (GEORGE HERBERT MEAD); WORLD CONSCIOUSNESS.

MORE WITH LESS.

MUSIC IS PERMANENT; ONLY LISTENING IS INTERMITTENT (THOREAU).

INVENTION.

Not things, but minds.

Dealing with 1, not 2.

To make a garden empty-minded.

Music = no music.

Inclusive, not exclusive: aperiodic; no vision, etc.

Objective within; going in all directions.

Demilitarization of language (no government).

A music that needs no rehearsal.

Feet on the ground.

To set all well afloat (Thoreau: Yes and No are lies. The only true answer will set all well afloat.).

Art's self-alteration.

Impossibility of repeated actions; loss of memory. To reach these two's a goal (Duchamp).

Complexity of nature; giving up simplicity of soul, vision, etc.

Constellation of ideas (five as a minimum).

Problems of music (vision) only solved when silence (non-vision) is taken as the basis.

Giving unto others what they wish to be given, not what you would wish to be given (alteration of the Golden Rule).

Use all solutions; do everything!

Inactivity (the camera).

Goal is not to have a goal.

This is one text in an ongoing series; to find a way of writing which though coming from ideas is not about them; or is not about ideas but produces them.

I used I Ching chance operations to find which of these ideas would be the subject of mesostics on which name. In this way I gradually developed a library of mesostics.

Instead of using them as text in their own right, I used them as material for renga. Renga is a classical form of Japanese poetry. Many people now know haiku, but not so many know renga, though Octavio Paz in collaboration with other western poets has written renga. A haiku in Japanese has no fixed meaning. Its words are not defined syntactically. Each is either noun, verb, adjective, or adverb. A group of Japanese of an evening can therefore entertain themselves by discovering new meanings for old haikus.

> matsutake ya
> shirano ho no ka no
> hebaritsuku

This is a poem by Bashō. Translated into nouns it is:

> pine mushroom
> ignorance leaf of tree
> adhesiveness

This is R.H. Blythe's translation:

> The leaf of some unknown tree
> Sticking
> On the mushroom.

I showed that to Toshi Ichiyanagi. He said: That is not a very interesting translation. I asked him how he would translate it. He said he'd think about it. Two days later he brought me:

Mushroom
Does not know leaf
Is sticking on it.

In the course of five or six years, having gotten the idea, I made two more:

That that's unknown
Brings mushroom and leaf
Together.

And, finally:

What mushroom?
What leaf?

From a strict point of view this last translation is not cricket, but the fact that the poem consists of questions rather than statements suggests ignorance and their juxtaposition suggests adhesiveness.

Haiku is short: five, seven, five syllables. Renga is long: five, seven, five; seven, seven expressed at least thirty-six times.

Traditionally renga is written by a group of poets finding themselves of an evening together and having nothing better to do. Successive lines are written by different poets. Each poet tries to make his line as distant in possible meanings from the preceding line as he can take it. This is no doubt an attempt to open the minds of the poets and listeners or readers to other relationships than those ordinarily perceived. In Buddhist thought all creation is a network of cause and effect: everything causes everything else; everything results from everything else. Buddhism is utterly ecological and that is one of the reasons it has attracted so many occidental followers in recent years. Since everything is nothing but cause and effect, Buddhists see that it is unnecessary or impossible to speak in terms of cause and effect. Thus an intentionally irrational poem can be written with liberating effect. This is called purposeful purposelessness. That renga is written by several poets conduces to its being free of the ego of any single one of them.

In Buddhist thought, mind goes full circle: out from the ego through sense perceptions to the world of relativity, around and down to the Absolute (what Eckhart called the Ground), back through what Jung called the Collective Unconscious, and then in through dreams to the ego. Suzuki said that the ego has the capacity in this full circle to cut itself off from its experience whether that comes from without through the senses or from within through the dreams. Or it has the capacity to flow with its experience. And Suzuki said, flowing full circle is what Zen wants.

Sitting and breathing is a discipline for starting the flow in an ingoing direction. And the Australian aborigines with whom Marina Abramovic/Ulay and Ulay will shortly be living for a year use their dreams for this same initiation.

Artists who use disciplines that free their work from their intentions start the flow moving in an outgoing direction. Renga is a social example.

I used my library of mesostics on one hundred and ten different subjects and fifteen different names to make a chance-determined renga-like mix. The first *Themes* were written for a symposium of artists on the island of Ponape in the South Pacific organized by Kathan Brown of the Crown Point Press in Oakland and by Tom Marioni, Director and Founder of the Museum of Conceptual Art in San Francisco. Each of the twelve artists had been asked to make a twelve minute text to be recorded and issued as *Vision IV*. The symposium was called *Word of Mouth* and took place during the third week of January 1980. The mouth is more important than we think. Just as one hundred people at Black Mountain College, and one hundred people at Emma Lake in Saskatchewan, so at Ponape thirty-five through eating their meals in the same room became a family. Life on earth can be improved by means of food alone.

In Ponape I got the idea to extend my twelve minute talk to an hour by performing the chance operations four more times on the same, or, where necessary, lengthened material. Where through chance operations I had too little space for the name of one of the themes, I used his initials. I have placed Roman numerals in the left margin and again in the Variations together with parentheses giving the position(s) of that theme in previous twelve minute section(s). In the right margin the time in minutes and seconds is given at regular intervals.

The lines that are to be read in a single breath are printed singly or together as a stanza. These divisions or liaisons were not chance-determined, but were arrived at by improvisational means.

To conclude this introduction I give the first part of all five mesostics on the name of David Tudor (David Tudor David) which were the material for the renga but which were not themselves the renga. And finally the corresponding parts of the finished mixed nonsyntactical text.

I

we Don't know

whAt

we'll haVe

when we fInish

Doing

whaT we're doing

bUt

we know every Detail

Of

pRocess

we're involveD in

A way

to leaVe no traces

nothIng in between

herDed ox

2

before stuDying
mountAin
and Valley
zen Is zen
while stuDying
mounTain
zen becomes confUsing
after stuDying
mOuntain
River
Desert
lAke
and Valley
zen Is zen
Difference

3

Dumb
At dawn
what i haVe
Is
all i neeD
excepT
for yoU
south sea islanD
shifting Of
mountain bReeze
sound of birDs
dArk
has giVen way
to lIght
no neeD

4

the white birDs
fly in pAirs
they haVe
thIngs
to Do
Together
that reqUire
Duality
they fly abOve
the tRees
now anD then descending
to An upper branch
whereVer they're
goIng is where
they've alreaDy landed

5

we Don't
reheArse together
we gaVe that up long ago
before we gave up smokIng
why Do people
sTill ask
qUestions
i finD it
Odd
stRange
when he quoteD something
i hAd said
it seemed to haVe
a lIttle value
but when i reaD
iT by myself
i mUst say
it seemeD
of nO use at all
buRn the books

we Don't know
At dawn
and Valley
thIngs
to Do

whaT we're doing

zen becomes confUsing
south sea islanD

mOuntain

mountain bReeze

Desert

lAke

to leaVe no traces
nothIng in between
no neeD

before stuDying
whAt
we'll haVe
zen Is zen

while stuDying
excepT

bUt
after stuDying

mOuntain

mountain bReeze

VARIATION II
                          we Don't know
                               At dawn
          what i haVe

                          zen Is zen

          all i neeD

                          mounTain
                          for yoU

          south sea islanD
                               Of
          mountain bReeze

                          sounDs of birds

                               A way
                          and Valley

                          zen Is zen

                          herDed ox

VARIATION III
                          we Don't
                          mountAin
                          we'll haVe
          when we fInish
                               to Do
                          whaT we're doing
                          for yoU

                          Duality

70

they fly abOve
mountain bReeze

Desert
lAke

whereVer they're
a lIttle value

Difference

the white birDs
reheArse together
they haVe

zen Is zen
while stuDying

sTill am

bUt
Duality
Odd
River

71

themes & variations

it was a Juncture
to go thAt way or this

Most
no longEr
doeSn't

it is Just
hOw

of the manY benefits
Coming to us

nErvous system

              past's Just
               whAt did you say

          clearing the Mind of music
               wE accept
     if i gave up my Sense of accomplishment
               and Just
               nOw
           of anYthing else

          we are in yuCatan
            out thE window   .244

II   were we Just
             elevAted

    or did we pull ourSelves
             uP

             thE
          even to youRself

             Just
           Obscure related
      you in form you Have
             iN a place
          that workS

III   transforMation
            to bE done

      have disappeaRed from daily life

                    they Can
                      bE seen

                    we Can   .488
                    measUre
                    its leNgth

                  divide it aNd
                     only If
                 there isN't any is there vision
        on their mailinG list
                      tHey send you
                      pArt
                  the saMe

              there isn't Much

                    somE
                   woRk
                     Can
                    bE found
                to be Complete
                   yoU are kept
                   iN
          about how the liNe   1.132
                     I
               drawN between the two

                 thus makinG it susceptible to divine influences
                    to tHe museum
                    to tAke out a rule

        just videophone for perMission

                            75

you can take out as Many
continuEd
as though i weRe no longer there
the deCision
sEe

that the Car
on oUr use
of eNergy
have beeN parked

memorIze
but i didN't   1.376

now and then we'd Go out
to sHop for lunch

or cAll
soMe people

find it too Much

stayEd

tRy to get the rules
i Could
havE
beCome
if yoU've
aNd i could have
by meaNs
or trIed
to fiNd some help
where we could Get some cous cous
sober stomacH   2.02

red tApe's connected

quiet Mind

if they seeM
to be the sAme

i enjoy heaRing from you

but maKe
The
such that it is nOt

By paying
thE stones
Years ago

i set My mind
thAt continues
foRever the sand

i maKe
iT is

each frOm the other

But

to rEconsider
generositY

writing Music

don't Add
beyond affiRmation beyond negation

2.264

Koan

a sudden crash of Thunder

the mind dOors
By many physicists
whitE to white

nothing's changed Yet
soMething immense

thAt adds up
to zeRo
to Keep me

There's
nO dust

its Biology   2.508

didn't want to hEar it in the first place

drY ink

there is no Mirror
And
youR ears
i Know

saTie

printed prOgram

But
no nEed

whY

                    tHis
soul is so simplE
            liviNg
    in a paRticular
    at anY one time

                    Do   3.152
            stArt with two

        i haVe
            Is
        he Does
        or Two

            tHeatre

        nO

    the woRds

    to havE it be

            Arise

            Utopia

        erewHon
    this vEry day

        seNses
    tomoRrow too

        waY way works

79

at first seemeD
        Another beginning
    to haVe
        of Its inhabitants
    anD
in a differenT way

        tHat will be
        One

        foR
        bE
            Afterwards
            Underground
        witH
        othErs

you see cloud iN sky

        oR notre dame
    in a final waY
        of sounD

        to tAke the final step

        riVulet
        happIly

i'll have in minD
        whaT
        tHe
    stretching Of the muscles

        eRasing
    to bE not there but here

previous yeAr

where is the mUsic

                Has
            thE same effect
    or did i turN away

            thRee four or five

            sYnergy

        i haD
            nArrows

    but i haVe not yet found   4.284
            Iceberg

        gooD condition

VI

My word

        thAt
            Rolling around

            Can you
        say somEthing
    but not cLearly

        not Dance

        withoUt
    unprediCtable
            wHy did you
    repeAt yourself just now

raMbling
Person
tell Me

dAnce and music   4.528
figuRe

it didn't Catch on

i bE
aLl their time
Dancing
groUnd?

to write musiC

notHing
hAd a chance to rest

is accoM-

accomPlished

Multiplicity

rAn
no play of poweR

danCing
frEe

in its own pLace

it coulD have been someone else   5.172

or soUth or north

Confusium
Hold them

this wAy and that

be Made by someone else

a haPpenıng

no need to Move
thAt coin

a memoRy
tranSfer

tHe need

sAme time

she is going to give a Lecture
to the peopLe up in boston

i think the Mind

Continue

move it aLl the time

that mUst   5.416
in tHe
right off the bAt

what is the differeNce

i have More
moving And not moving

eveR

chance operationS
or tHe feelings
thAt
Look
aLl over
alMost immediately

but the intelleCt
by identifying himseLf
qUite
tHe other film
thAt shows
traNsferring
i Move
A keystone comedy

otheR the memory imprint
exiSts

How
to reAch
the impossibiLity of transferring
from one Like object to another
that Made a habit
to reaCh
doesn't have to foLlow
optimUm surface quality

patH

A help

6.06

suzuki chaNged my mind thirty-two years ago

highest purpose Be
                        dUst

                            Camera   6.304

                    now we Know
                what coMes
                    to It

                    Not moving

            he received thoSe
                highesT
                solvE

                    duRation did it
        and on the same Floor next door

                        measUrements
                with Less dust

                    smaLl
                        dEtails
                            fReed music from its rules

                he said i Breathe

            work withoUt work

                              aCt
                                liKe nature   6.548
                            if we Must
                            otherwIse
                            earth iN
                                Spring
                              as Though
              following his advicE
              he had gone undeRground

                                Feeling

                  knew what was Up

                                Life
                            on a cLoud

                            lovE
                            befoR'hand

        IX   didn't know what wE
                                weRe

                  place attentIon

                          maKïng behavior   7.192

                        no deSire no dislike
                      with pleAsure

                  or do you find iT
                          producIng
                          laughtEars

both of thEm
is Rearrange

tIme

King
to what haSn't
is fAce
noT
Is about

it workEd
and Enlightenment
maRked on map

I   7.43⁶
asK
yourSelf

is there Any need
for governmenT

It works
as wEll
nEed
betteR
to be wIthout

quicK
Sound of children

A
waTer

superfIcial
aspEcts

fixEs itself

boRedom
or I
worK   8.o8

Stones
And
unemploymenT

from heIght
rEgrets

x   thus fiNally
the image On
     as faR as we can te
i was deeply iMpressed

thAt's
Needed's
fOrgotten

unattainaBle goal

consideR
everybOdy
the Widow
to remaiN closed   8.324
or to opeN itself

tO

with *aRia*

i left the list at hoMe in new york
               thAt were

will be arraNged

in san diegO

               has Been will be
          that woRks

     intermissiOns
                    Will be
                    Naturally
what we haveN't
necessarily gOt

               incReased time and space

               More
          so thAt   8.568
               thaN less

                    Of the pieces will be known
          an oBstacle

               Ram's
               Or superimposition
          forWard

     woodeN

     happeNed

nO

thRee

Most questions

roAratorio

aN evening

oRigin
is hOw it's now

But
thEse
bRings
To be accepted
those aRe
trAck assignment
is eqUal
loudneSs

stereo loCation

morpHology
couldn't bE heard

chaNge the music

But
thEy
would be betteR off without her

beGin with
embRace

but it will take a lOng time
inaBility
my guEss   9.456
befoRe
Ten
to woRk
to strAighten

it's aUdible

their liveS
he aCquired
His
off thE press
News

their Birthdays
Each day
of ouR
chanGe the minds

news we ouRselves
cOmplete

aBout
rEmaining   10.10
twenty-one otheRs
Than
obscuRe

lAw
cUt up to make
a reServoir

Crime
witHout him

Equal
atteNtion
in comBination
arE

dRy points

what's aGainst it

engRavings

nOise
Burnt
spacE to time   10.344

oR
of Theory

XII   experience is a forM

cOmplexity

paRalysis

extRemes
your mInd

that'S what
Goes
faR
And
now it's obVious
gEtting rid of them

92

muSt
see world as Mind
revOlution

no conceRn
to change the woRld
wIth view
viSion

XIII

A
look at woRld
aNarchy is practical

yOu
by peopLe
anD
Sound
to Care
for tHe
any wOrd
of Earth

aNother
possiBility
of succEss

alteR

no Gloom
insteAd of syntax
suRprise

everythiNg
between gOod
an aLphabet

life Death

XIV
we Don't know
At dawn
and Valley
thIngs
to Do

whaT we're doing

zen becomes confUsing
south sea islanD

mOuntain

mountain bReeze   11.476

Desert

lAke

to leaVe no traces
nothIng in between
no neeD

XV
curioSity
extenDed

no uSe

no minDedness   12.00
I (VII)   no need to Move   (SLOWER)

thAt coin

94

a memoRy

Side
He
sAme time

she is going to give a Lecture
to the peopLe up in boston

the saMe   12.1469
Changes
move it aLl the time
that mUst
in tHe
right off the bAt
let it daNce

we get through tiMe
thAn
and destRoying it

chance operationS

the sHots

i cAn
he no Longer
has any connection at aLl

II (IX)   comEdy

gReatest of arts

studyIng being interrupted

i asK you
do you anSwer telephone
with pleAsure
follows Thunderclap
producIng
an intErruption
what you havE to do

pResence

your mInd

King

abSence
hAppened
unexpecTed
salvatIon
Exotic
spEcies
samsaRa
Interrupted
asK
yourSelf

A
for governmenT
of short-cIrcuiting
any furthEr
thE

i pRefer
to be wIthout
liKe
diScover
essentiAls

being independenT of both
Is
aspEcts

III (XII)   Multiplicity
whO

faR in
aiRport   13.4283

In
oppoSites

what was he thinkinG of when
faR
simultAneously
haVing
not Enough
muSt
see world as Mind

revOlution
as day's woRk
niRvana

practIcal
of Self to self
Going

extRemes

fAilure

haVing 14.1221
hopE
iS
theM
in a harmOny
otheRs
Room
by one hundred fIfty
So that what's out
can Get
helicopteR

A circus

and now the Violin
of such nEgative
of one muSic all alone

i aM glad
tO have

it is not only moRe

the tangRam book 14.4159

automatIcally
of wayS

chanGing
Removed
the vAriety
Vitality

naturE
comeS
   froM it
      bOth full and empty
   destRoyed
by fiRe

      stIll
writing muSic
or even writinG this
   my woRk
      past And present

      Viaduct   15.1097
of a changEd
      beSt
         Mankind
         Of
      fuRther selflessness

      aRt

   honorIng it
and what'S called art

IV (I)   is it Just
                  whAt do you think about the future
   boredoM

      Every mind
   knowS thought about it's
      disJunct's

hOw
of the manY benefits
to musiC
himsElf   15.4035

        past's Just
            As unstable

        My
        bE invented
if i gave up my Sense of accomplishment
what'd you Just
anything in frOnt
    without anY waiting
we are in yuCatan
            and Every unpredicted thing
                i Just couldn't
            to whAt you've said
            but i aM
                hEaring
            with itSelf

v (x)   thus fiNally
                            Of   16.0973
                        electRonic
                        reMedy

                    plurAlity
                    of ceNters

                    cOmposed

                    we are aBout
                        but oRdinary daily life
                            Of my music
                            World
                    forever aNd

vi (v)   do unto otHers

                            winDow
                            beTween good and evil

vii (xiii)   wAy to think
                    in a place that woRks

                            gettiNg rid
                                Of this idea
                            to compLete the circle
                    with no one leaDing   16.3811

viii (iii)   Many
                            rulEs
                    have disappeaRed from daily life

                            they Can
                                sEe
                        on miCrofilm
                            Use

                        there is No
                            Need
                        only If

                    but i didN't

101

Going
'round tHe world

All
theM   17.0749

i siMply
thE automobile was
no longeR there

Can
bE borrowed
and others Can't
had no Use for it just had it
iN
their possessioN
I
to fiNd some help
lookinG for it
as tHough
i hAd parked it
in othersoMe place

we got up early each Morning
at onE time   17.3687

long houRs
the work Could not
that thE work
we Can

on oUr use
its leNgth
though we didN't work
avaIlable time

102

in five secoNds are yours

now and then we'd Go out
giving eacH
is whAt's difficult
soMe people

aMount
of attEntion

tRy to get the rules
baCk

thEn be   18.0625
Complete

to the hoUse
Not yet
by meaNs

the purpose of musIc
you caN't
thus makinG it susceptible to divine influences
everytHing
explAined

quiet Mind

IX (XI)   i neveR did it

and hOrizontally

frame By
inclusivE
aRe
To be accepted
oR
not to be Accepted   18.3563

Unfortunately
muSt
of Course
is wHat

bEcause
of the movemeNt of the cleaning women
Bubbling
thEy
Reducing
they'll Get even
to the length of a shoRt
was a cOpy of another
invisiBly
thE sand
fRom
Ten

x (vi)   what did you have in Mind
when you sAid instantaneous   19.0501

men aRe men

eaCh

rEmember
just a Little

              not Dance
           withoUt
           musiC

              wHy did you
           repeAt yourself just now

              Men are men as before

              Put yourself

           tell Me
           whAt
        you aRe not on wheels

              i Can't

              thE dancers were spending
              a Little   19.3439
     off the grounD
           groUnd

              Can't you see
           notHing
              hAd a chance to rest

        is accoM-
              Peace
        their Minds

           rAn
     no play of poweR

              Composing
           frEe

no accompLishment's
involveD

yoUr ears
are exCellent

Hold them
this wAy and that   20.0377

Moving
Play

it still seeMs to me
speAking
you aRe
putting on orange Cloth

mEditation

the Little trap
that noboDy
aboUt
i Can't quite
for awHile
whAt you're saying

raMakrishna
of Place

coMes
indiA

Re-   20.3315

refleCt

wE say
we go to the same pLace

i'll go Down

i sUppose she's right

inseCurity
in Her
dAy
will becoMe
a Pupil

XI (II)   Just
pregnAnt fluent
or did we pull ourSelves
on the Part of
is possiblE
even to youRself
of Just what happened   21.0253

lOse connection

anarcHy

flyiNg
that workS

Just high
And
the Same
Piano

107

mutEd

Rumor

obJect

peOple
High
aNd
whiStling

obJect
exActly   21.3191
to uSe of fossil fuels

Playing
Echo
of thundeR

xii (xv)   mind'S
aND attention
for meaningS
for value juDging

xiii (iv)   we coMe
to the sAnd

no Regrets

we Know
enTertainment
Or not
and Backwards

thE stones
impermanentlY

the naMe   22.0129
of the stAtion
foRever the sand
is what we finally looK
iT is
tO find out what's going on now

But
by rElationship
generositY
as Music
hAs nothing to do with
beyond affiRmation beyond negation

Koan
or aT least
yOu
By many physicists
opEn

exactlY how   22.3067
i reMember
wAs played
to zeRo
that we didn't have to Know
where The ticket is
is related tO the music

a Basic list
if sEntient

a thoroughlY planned
for different Men

just A single
aRound
always looKing
saTie
printed prOgram

But
thE two

whY

she gave Me the book
the other detAils escape
with each peRson
Knowing
one of The
tO nothing
the Blank
had nEver heard
for one two or three Years

his coMment

thAt isn't the way it goes

he's theRe waiting for her
didn't Know what to say

23.0005

XIV (VIII)   By remaining silent
where yoU are

as Child
to Know nothing of destruction   23.2943

he had More than one
I

oNe in which
viSion's
highesT
whEn
the dust was theRe

xv (xiv)   before stuDying
whAt
we'll haVe
zen Is zen

while stuDying
excepT

bUt
after stuDying

mOuntain

mountain bReeze   24.00

I (v, vi)   meister eckHart   (FASTER; APPROX. 1ST TEMPO)
whEre you are

liviNg
will aRise
to find its waY

                    Discipline
                 whAt you're doing
             get to fiVe

          move that Is from music alone
       to music anD dance from music and dance
                    To
                 elsewHere

                    Of
                 this oR that
             it's its othEr side

                    As
                 facUlties
                 erewHon
                 of thE   24.2454
                    seNses
             tomoRrow too

             waY way works

       at first seemeD
                    Another beginning

             to haVe
                agaIn
                   Differences are

ɪɪ (xɪɪ, ɪɪɪ)   Man
                 whO
                 paRalysis
             betteR to change

             turnIng invention

                    the Sky

what was he thinkinG of when
            lawyeRs
            simultAneously   24.4908
      now it's obVious
                  gEtting rid of them

                    So
        is quite another Matter

                  revOlution
            has Room within

              wheReas
              gIft
              of Self to self

              Going
              accoRding to
              And
      without haVing
            no schEdule
      the endingS one can study the openings
            the Middle game
                  fOolish   25.1362

              moRe
              dRama

I
ham Sandwiches
makinG it possible
Resist
A circus
of Various musics
to takE the place
of one muSic all alone

i aM glad
tO have
familiaR
peRhaps
It
iS

beinG   25.3816
the woRd
tAken away

seemingly Vast

to thE next

haS it
froM it
withOut it
has both memoRy
we aRe lost
I mean by me
becomeS continuation

III (III, VIII)   plants exeMplify
continuEd
have disappeaRed from daily life

no Climax

no argumEnt

full Circle
is difficUlt   26.0270
iNto the world

Not to be moved
where I parked it

but i didN't

Going
He knew it
by heArt

in My
i was Making
thE automobile was
no longeR there

Casual
hEat

iv (xv, xii)   what iS
yoUr problems
that our plans minimiZe
Unabated   26.2714

we maKe efforts
I
silence of course Doesn't exist

A
of operatIon
not So to
Experienced
facT

it Zeroed in
with abSence
whatever yoU give them to do

they materialiZe
spiritUal
lacK
facultIes

Decide

thAt's to say   26.5168

on the vacatIon

infrared rayS

so that thE
life and deaTh
gaZing

Someone
Unify

disappears beyond horiZon

makes Unpredictable
with no Knowledge
fermentatIon

he nameD them
in whAtever's
happenIng

floweringS
ablE

i Thank   27.1622
demagnetiZation

when you realize it iS
to their langUage
Zany

yoU
that guy could maKe
electrostatIcs

i wonDer
what then is the importAnce
one thIng
will toeS

if thE average person
Toe nails have

social horiZon

v (ix, ii)   what did you mEan
                      when you said you weRe
                                studyIng being interrupted   27.4076
                                liKe
                        do you anSwer telephone
                                lAugh
                    or did you find iT
                            producIng
                        an intErruption
                  what you havE to do

                              pResence

                        churchIs a rule

                            maKe it open
                            abSence
                            hAppened

                            noT
                        salvatIon
                      to happEn
                          thEn

                        kept aRound   28.043
                    for tourIst trade

                  you're unKnotted
                        yourSelf
                    other wAy around

                                  118

meThod
It works
thE
thE
i pRefer
whatIs

providing utilities worK

iS slow
And
parT
superfIcial
aspEcts

wE
theRefore   28.2884
profIt
one bricK

queStions
promote peAce
wiThout
self securIty
commitmEnt
wE

no locked dooR

wIll be
bacK and forth

hiS own
who wAs

going norTh

I
lifE

vi (xi, ix) how was it befoRe

taking care Of children
is Busy

thEse
pRecise
aTtention

those aRe
not to be Accepted

relative dUration

She thinks
her Care
is wHat
hEr
chaNge the music
Bubbling
thE
goveRnment
he was hopinG
that the pictuRe   29.1792
tO japan
inaBility

my guEss
fRom
Ten

120

heaRing's
At the time
whatever's Unformed

Seeing's
he aCquired

wHat

idEas
oN
aBout
thE condition

ability's enviRonment
Goes   29.4246

VII (VII, I)   she is giving Me
shiAtsu

we aRe talking
aS ever
tHe need
to dAnce
onLy then

aLive

no need to Move

Changes
Later or before

that mUst
be anotHer
choreogrAphy

let it daNce

between Mind
moving And not moving

an aRt   30.07
for the Soul
or tHe feelings
thAt
quickLy when the body changes
obLige observer

there are Mushrooms
any plaCe
by identifying himseLf with
yoU
migHt
wAy

what actually happeNed

i used to think the Mind
wAs
sepaRate from the body
exiSts
it was tHought

cAn   30.3154
haLt
be caLled

VIII (VI, X)   anonyMity

thAt
the puRpose

122

eaCh
say somEthing

just a Little

anD
instantaneoUs and
then i Came back

How

Afterwards
Men are men as before

Put yourself
one art More
situAtion   30.5608

you aRe saying
it didn't Catch on

figurE
how it reLates to anonymity

IX (II, XI)   rose, nail or Just string

pregnAnt; fluent

or did we pull ourSelves
i hadn't Put
into thE
on my wRist

don't Just

a little mOre
you in form you Have

plaN
that workS
less Judgment
And
or thoughtleSsness

divisive Politics
takEn

youngeR ones must do it

x (VIII, XIV)

Brighten the corner
withoUt one
Creation

maKe
to be coMpletely
studIo

oNe in which
he received thoSe
noT
thE
the dust was theRe

iF

sUch me

aLready
see it in aLl
bE
in which he continued his woRk

he said i Breathe

bUt

and musiCian

also worK
         to Make people take you
         serIously

earth iN
     iS
he was jusT
think i didn't givE

         no pRodding no poking

     Feeling
knew what was Up

         Life   32.097
     on a cLoud
     for thE

                   oR putting them on
xi (xiii, vii)   wAy to think
     in a place that woRks

         goverNment
     turned rOund

         Light
with no one leaDing

125

dancerS
Can be dropped
like tHe
any wOrd

thE others
to humaN needs

possiBility
Exemplified   32.3424

pResent instance

no Government

XII (I, IV)   Just
educAtion

My
Everyone

i waS making music

it is Just
One
bY listening
Coming to us
sincE we changed our minds

a Juncture

whAt did you say

My
so that thE
if i gave up my Sense of accomplishment
and Just   32.5878
nOw
without anY waiting
to eaCh
shE looks up and smiles

Just
this yeAr she died

Making my mind
in hEr world

elSe would be equal sense

xiii (iv, xiii)   if they seeM

pleAse

no Regrets

but maKe
is iT changing
stOnes are there

an oBligation

a littlE attention   33.2332
to replY

the naMe
At ease
foR which they have no taste

127

i maKe
aT
and hOw it puts you to sleep

expends itself in streams But
not as nEws

acts in the same waY

blowing a troMbone
hAs nothing to do with
eRase
chess lacKs

xiv (x, v)   miNd's
Of
electRonic   33.4786
has been deterMined
thAt's
Needed's
cOmposed?

we are aBout
to make a ciRcus
Of my music
not Withheld
from aNy form of life

suNsmell

fOntana mix
with *aRia*

world a Meeting house
thAt is
Nature
Of nature

world must Be something

i'm faiRly sure   34.124
therefOre
that doesn't Work
takiNg place
that ruNs
smOothly
the stage if theRe is one
will be eMpty
rAther
thaN less

encOunter

we Believe
in eveRything
Or superimposition

a single piece Will be played
accordiNg
to chaNce
at hOme

Regrets   34.3694

Most questions
Are
obstructioN free

the questiOn now is
But
a ceRtain
they've been taught nOt to rehearse

What more
caN you say

xv (xiv, xv)   we Don't know
At dawn
what i haVe

zen Is zen

all i neeD

mounTain
for yoU

south sea islanD   35.0648
Of
mountain bReeze

sounDs of birds

A way
and Valley

zen Is zen

herDed ox

whaT difference
walked throUgh

finD a difference

wOuld you say
youR feet
are a little off the grounD

sAy
to leaVe no traces

Important
to have your heaD
To fall   35.3102

bUt
no one Disturbed him he slept

nO one knew
aRe sure your feet
anD legs
reAdy

leaVe
posItions

a Dance

a vacaTion

zen is no longer confUsing
after stuDying
frOm time to time

put the otheR back on the hook

he saiD
rengA
because of the Very great
dIfferences   35.5556
Drive
Than
yoU
in my minD
i shOuld

spRingweather springweather   36.00

i (iv, xiii, xiii)   My   (faster)
to be the sAme

of how natuRe
we Know
That
stOnes are there

By paying
whEn
theY

the eMptiness

thAt continues
in heR manner of operation   36.1516
i maKe

They're actually separate

laO-tse
made Blind

continuE

acts in the same waY

writing Music
in imitAtion
beyond affiRmation beyond negation
as it was Known
or aT least
yOu
By many physicists
opEn

nothing's changed Yet
soMething immense
Asking   36.3790

guntheR stent

to Keep me
au couranT
is nO dust

a Basic list
of magazinEs

drY ink

there is no Mirror
And
we aRe
i Know

he gave me such a lisT

133

printed prOgram
row B

invEntion

whY

the bulletin of atoMic science   37.0064

strAvinsky
conceRt
with no lacK
one of The
tO fill out
the Blank

wE remain
for one two or three Years

II (III, VIII, III)   Many
rulEs
into poetRy

no Climax

no argumEnt

that the Car
shoUld
Not
possessioN
where I parked it   37.2338
but i didN't

Going
tHey send you
by stAying where we are
the inforMation

there isn't Much

somE
wheRe i was
Couldn't
bE found

beCome
anxioUs
aNd i could have
about how the liNe
or trIed
weNt on

you don't have to Go
as tHough   37.4612
i hAd parked it

Moved to the other side of the bed

we got up early each Morning
at onE time
as you can Remember

the work Could not
whEn you hear the tone

you have to speak quiCkly

135

measUre
as maNy rules
though we didN't work
avaIlable time
i Never do
into cateGories
giving eacH
pArt
the evening Meal

38.0896

we walked froM
attEntion

tRy to get the rules
and eaCh

thEn be

III (xv, xii, iv)   the way to Solve
yoUr problems
is to locate their Zero

woUldn't
we maKe efforts
to Imitate her
in her Depths

but that doesn't meAn
of operatIon

                    not So to
                 spEak superficially
        from underneaTh   38.317
                    it Zeroed in
              on proceSs
                of yoUr intention

              sympathiZe
                to mUsic

                    Know
                 aIr

                    Decide

                 thAt's to say

        on the vacatIon

        infrared rayS

              fossil fuEls

                 lighT

                 bliZzard

              tornadoeS
                 engUlfed you

                 wiZard
              makes Unpredictable   38.5444

                       137

with no Knowledge
fermentatIon
        Deliquescence
in whAtever's
happenIng

floweringS

phosphorEscence
momenT

demagnetiZation
      She said
   as thoUgh
    wiZard

   yoU
    Know
electrostatIcs
     tiDes
    spAce
    tIme   39.1718
    Sun
   algaE

    Toe nails have
nothingness horiZon

what he Said
will interest yoU no matter who you are

the utiliZation
of compUter and mind as duo

138

blacK and blue toes
and dIslikes

IV (X, V, XIV)   coexisteNce
nOw
as faR as we can tell

reMedy

plurAlity
Needed's
sOcial not individual

an unattainaBle goal   39.3992
to make a ciRcus
abOut the ego

the Widow
to remaiN closed

giviNg
attentiOn
and fouRth
or to dreaMs

world A meeting house
will be arraNged
Of nature
has Been will be
i'm faiRly sure

nOt something
otherWise

Naturally
at uNexpected times

sO   40.0266

a stRing
will be eMpty

rAther
they Never

Organ

Bubbles
in eveRything

hOrn

a single piece Will be played

accordiNg
beNch

nO
Regrets

Moon

Atlas

aN evening

it seems tOo much to ask

oBlige
a ceRtain
renunciatiOn of likes and dislikes

of What
caN you say

turNs
questiOn

Redouble

asked Me
they hAve
did i believe iN it
but gOod intentions

if i don't Believe in magic
anotheR
persOn
and War
is Nonsense

v (i, iv, xii)

it was a Juncture

educAtion

without My
Everyone
i waS making music

it is Just
that i accOmplish so much
You

40.254

40.4814

                    Coming to us
                    himsElf

                    we reJect
                        whAt did you say
            clearing the Mind of music
                    bE invented
                    electronicS and
                    what'd you Just
                    the limitatiOns of the mind

            not a realitY independent of it

                    an aneChoic   41.1088
                    in that rEvision that invention

                        Just
                        thAt will decide
                        of My
                        hEaring
                        near Samoa

there are those who think i'm Jesting
                    thOugh i'm not

                        theY
                            Can it
                        abilitiEs
                            Joking seriously
            even when thAt joy
                        her Many
                        thE

            count baSie in his seventies

not a funny Jest   41.3362
the decisiOn
base all the laws on povertY
plaCing imagination
livE with happily

these interruptions are Just
for eAch and everyone

went froM calais

accEptance
aS i need

i Just made
Open mind
but easilY altered mistake

no politiCians

no policE

Just
tAking
Much
morE time   41.5636
of Smiling

vi (ii, xi, ix)   were we Just
A little
moveS in all directions
on the Part of
is possiblE
even to youRself

Just
lOse connection
witH earth

that secoNd taken
our way of nowneSs

Just high
And
leSs
divisive Politics
mutEd
Rumor

42.191

Just
shOrt
High
aNd
of ownerShip

obJect
to wAr

the Same
Playing

Echo
of thundeR

Just
cOmplexity

Have a dream

eNter

underStand

Just   42.4184
less lAw

i went to See the gliding
but the wind had been Put
in thE
wRong direction
aboriginal Judgment
as we dO or used to do

Have a dream

dad Never kept a car

into everyone'S life

Just
one yeAr
how long Shall
we keeP
shE gave me
aRe they ours

anonyMity

the clAss   43.0458
was a veRy long time ago
of my writing musiC was
say somEthing
just a Little
not Dance
with soUnds
unprediCtable

                    wHy did you
                    mAde
               by the saMe
                    Perhaps twenty-five

VIII (XII, III, II)   experience is a forM
                        far Out

                    the stoRy
                      betteR to change
                      turnIng invention
                    into Spoilsport

what was he thinkinG of when   43.2732
                    thRee times
                    Away
                    haVing
                    wE
                    noteS
               having too Many

                    nO end
                    oveRnight

                    wheReas
                    practIcal
                    viSion
          we are on the verGe of success
                    oR
                    fAilure

                    haVing
                    lEarned
               of doing So   43.5006

146

Making
rOom

Remaining lost

suRrounded
I
it clear what'S what

even a Game
helicopteR
but it meAns
the mind an empty Van
onE étude after another
by the eyeS and ears

Makes
being lOst

Received

i Remember
more radIcal
not on the edgeS

44.1280

IX (IX, II, V)   didn't know what wE
gReatest of arts
doIng
i asK you
Seem in line

rAdical change

iT
not that, Is
invEntion

147

naturE

spoilspoRt

tIme

King
iS
eAch day
unexpecTed
salvatIon

it workEd

thEn
samsaRa
for tourIst trade

tanK
it'S
you hAve
for governmenT
of short-cIrcuiting
as wEll
to morE

betteR
to be wIthout
quicK
thiS

essentiAls
being independenT of both

44.3554

rIppling   44.5828
aspEcts
of sociEty

waR
Is then
bacK and forth
outSide

promote peAce

To get
In

commitmEnt

x (xiii, vii, xi)   mAcrobiotic
are the Same

xi (xi, ix, vi)   how was it befoRe
is hOw it's now

is Busy
and in timE to come
mind not sobeR
aTtention   45.2102
woRk to do
not to be Accepted

relative dUration
muSt

stereo loCation

morpHology

ignoranceE
childreN need

Bubbling

thE
suRface of the sphere

he was hopinG
embRace
tO japan
Budging
thE sand

befoRe
here To   45.4376

xii (v, vi, i)   river Has
facE

's'goNe to ocean
aRms
to find its waY

Discipline
grAdually disappeared

eVen
a versIon in which
he Does
iT
elsewHere

nO
veRsion

it's its othEr side
is An

Utopia

H
of thE

46.065

mahayaNa
tomoRrow too

and the daY after

an introDuction
And
need to Vary
wIth
Differences are
insTead of
wHat

One
paRt
bE

whAt's
mUsic
witH
dEsire
you see cloud iN sky

46.2924

Rain

foggY
Dew

mountAin stream

eVer
Inlet
Doing

or up and abouT

batH

the thOught of coming home

spRing
to bE not there but here
previous yeAr

where is the mUsic
tHat is
hEre
or did i turN away   46.5198
theRe
daY

XIII (XIV, XV, XV)   we Don't
mountAin
we'll haVe
when we fInish
to Do
whaT we're doing
for yoU

Duality

they fly abOve
mountain bReeze

Desert
lAke

whereVer they're
a lIttle value

Difference   47.1472

whaT difference

it mUst have been
t seemeD
nO
coveRing

are a little off the grounD

As she said

but Very much
In
snow continueD
in socieTy

Up it is to bolivia
your boDy
by fOod

aRms
are still on the grounD
one of them Answered

conVoluted   47.3746
posItions

                          your heaD

xiv (vii, i, vii)   no need to Move

                          aMmunition out of language

xv (viii, xiv, x)   he led us to Believe
                          withoUt one
                          Camera

                          maKe
                          what coMes

                          studIo

                          problems No one
                          of quieScence
                          To
                          sEe him

          the dust was theRe   48.00

i (iv, xiii, xiii, i)   we coMe   (slowly)
                          understAnding   48.0387
                          of how natuRe
                          we Know
                          That
                          nOw

                          But
                          a littlE attention
                          theY
                          the eMptiness

thAt continues

foreveR the sand
i maKe

ii (i, iv, xii, v)   is it Just
in the fAct that
My
Every mind
doeSn't
disJunct's   48.3483

One
of the manY benefits
teaChing
i can't bElieve it

we adJust
ourselves to dAily life
Must
Everything
every Single minute

and Just
paid attentiOn

not a realitY independent of it

present's double-headed present Consists
and Every unpredicted thing

i Just couldn't

this yeAr she died

155

but i aM
idEntical   49.0579
with itSelf

if we Just

what put the thOught

casuallY

Can it
havE been life

Just
even when thAt joy
My
sidEd life
had no deathS in it

III (IX, II, V, IX)   didn't know what wE
when you said you weRe

superfIcial controls

what result'ld be liKe

Seem in line

lAugh

or did you find iT   49.3675
not that, Is
an intErruption

naturE
of the pRocess

your mInd
liKed
abSence

eAch day
inTroduced
salvatIon
ignorancE

dEstination
maRked on map
Is nirvana

you're unKnotted
yourSelf

is there Any need   50.0771

Then
It works
as wEll

nEed
i pRefer
where we were goIng

quicK

IV (XI, IX, VI, XI)   how was it befoRe
taking care Of children
is Busy

mind unquiEt

mind not sobeR

To be accepted

woRk to do

technology's Absence or presence

Unfortunately

muSt
of Course   50.3867

wHat
hEr
caN now

But
morE

would be betteR off without her

they'll Get even

they aRe three

Of
By
spacE to time

oR have
Ten

theRe

or speAk
whatever's Unformed
inSide
unmusiCal   51.0963

wHat
idEas
oN
against aBility
any mEans
that they will eveR
Goes

one moRe buddha
rOund it

aBout
rEmaining

they aRe
as quieT
obscuRe
And
actUally
Smiling   51.4059

nature was Complete
paying to eacH
outsidE it
yes aNd no are lies

will make their futures Bright

mobilE

                    shoRter than mother
                    takinG his place

v (xii, iii, ii, viii)   experience is a forM
                              cOmplexity

                    the stoRy
                    botheRs no one

                    turnIng invention
                    oppoSites
        what was he thinkinG of when
                    faR
                    And
                    haVing   52.1155

        working whilE

                    muSt
        having too Many

                    Outside
        as day's woRk

                    niRvana

                    endIng
                    inSecurity

        up all niGht

                    oR

And
haVing
hopE

the endingS one can study the openings

soMe days
tO be found
Remaining lost

suRrounded   52.4251
for It

So that what's out

even a Game

foR
but it meAns
Various musics
to takE the place

feelingS
eMpty

being lOst

Received

peRhaps
It
getS in

but near the underlyinG
Removed
of chAnge

Visibly and audibly   53.1347
to gEt up

comeS
but reMembering what it was

hOuse
has both memoRy

with it we find ouRselves
I mean by me

becomeS continuation

is facilitatinG
futuRe
in a strAit jacket

haVing
all at oncE
changeS

VI (II, XI, IX, VI)   rose, nail or Just string
A little

or did we pull ourSelves
no rePort   53.4443

long ago into thE
goveRnment
of Just what happened

lOse connection
witH earth

flyiNg
that workS
less Judgment
And
Short
Piano

on account of thE change

poetRy

obJect

shOrt

tHe
laNd
whiStling   54.1539

obJect
exActly
the Same
riPpling
Echo

some woRk to do

Just
cOmplexity

i Have
No way

Socially pansocially

vii (vi, x,   what did you have in Mind
  viii, vii)

whAt
the puRpose
  Can you

at cEnter
beLl rings

viii (viii, xiv, x, xv)   it must Be a discovery   54.4635
    to Find interruptions
that Burn

Follow the air

ix (x, v, xiv, iv)   he had drawN
nOw

dissimilaRs
reMedy

thAt's
of ceNters
  fOrgotten
we are aBout

but oRdinary daily life

hOnor
not Withheld
forever aNd
  Nature's part

attentiOn   55.1931

the woRd outside

world a Meeting house

quAlity
is Nature
Of nature

world must Be something
that woRks

intermissiOns
We

Naturally

x (xv, xii, iv, iii)   the way to Solve
                                more Useful
                    that our plans minimiZe

                              yoU can solve any musical problem
                    when you thinK
                              to Imitate her
                              anD immobility is
                but that doesn't meAn   55.5027
                              underlyIng principle

                    what exiSts
                         is thE mind

                    ancienT overview

                it can sympathiZe
                    with abSence

as thoUgh
sympathiZe
to mUsic
lacK

aIr

XI (III, VIII, III, II)   the dreaM
rulEs
into poetRy
they Can
sEe

dad's adviCe
is difficUlt   56.2123

Not
possessioN
to vIsit them
sileNt
smilinG

tHey send you
All
why was he angry with Me
dreaM

somE
no longeR there
Can
havE
poliCe

yoU are kept

Now

their possessioN   56.5219

          or trIed
          drawN between the two

          lookinG for it
            as tHough
            to tAke out a rule
    in othersoMe place

XII (v, vi, i, xii)   smile on His
                          whEre you are

                  liviNg
        have moRe than one idea
            at anY one time

                  Doing
            grAdually disappeared

            so riVer
              Is
            to Do
              iT   57.2315
            elsewHere

                  Of
                veRsion
        it's its othEr side

              ideAs

              Utopia

eacH
c E

aNd

to undeRstand
exclusivitY

anD then comes the end

tower of bAbel

eVery one
wIth
visiteD
in a differenT way

wHat   57.5411
tO
appeaR

bE
so thAt
whether Underground
witH
dEsire

suggestioN of silence

Roaratorio

i am absolutelY certain
no matter what i Do
thAn
eVer
Is

whether Dreaming
whaT
it Has

Of   58.2507
its own vibRation

to be not thEre but here

wAterfall

isthmUs

xiii (vii, i, vii, xiv)   My purpose is to get out
the caMera

pictures coMe to it

xiv (xiii, vii, xi, x)   A
look at woRld
arouNd
turned rOund

to compLete the circle
Drawn

169

Sound
Can be dropped
for tHe
neither fOllowing
thE others   58.5603

No composer

But
Exemplified
foR all humanity

i am usinG them
insteAd of syntax

suRprise

everythiNg
wOrking

an aLphabet

Daily life
a buddhiSt
in order to get to the Core

Have
any relatiOn

arE
iN the world
to which you're Blind   59.2699
idEa
about the aiR

Generous

to find A way
no one obstRucts
iN which

Other

Like

feelings is what she saiD

xv (xiv, xv, xv, xiii)　　　the white birDs
reheArse together
they haVe

zen Is zen
while stuDying

sTill am

bUt
Duality　　　　　　　　59.5795
Odd
River　　　　　　　　　60.00

selected exact change titles

guillaume apollinaire
The Heresiarch & Co.
The Poet Assassinated

louis aragon
Paris Peasant
The Adventures of Telemachus

antonin artaud
Watchfiends & Rack Screams

leonora carrington
The Hearing Trumpet

giorgio de chirico
Hebdomeros & other writings

joseph cornell
Joseph Cornell's Dreams

salvador dalí
Oui

morton feldman
Give My Regards to Eighth St.

alice james
The Death and Letters of Alice
  James

alfred jarry
Exploits & Opinions of
  Dr. Faustroll, Pataphysician
The Supermale

franz kafka
The Blue Octavo Notebooks

lautréamont
Maldoror & the complete works

gérard de nerval
Aurélia & other writings

fernando pessoa
The Book of Disquiet
The Education of the Stoic

pablo picasso
The Burial of the Count of
  Orgaz & other poems

raymond roussel
How I Wrote Certain
  of My Books

kurt schwitters
PPPPPP

philippe soupault
Last Nights of Paris

gertrude stein
Everybody's Autobiography

stefan themerson
Bayamus & Cardinal Pölätüo

denton welch
In Youth is Pleasure
A Voice Through a Cloud
Maiden Voyage

unica zürn
Dark Spring

exact change 5 brewster street, cambridge, ma 02138 www.exactchange.com